All About Animals
Ducks

By Christina Wilsdon

Reader's Digest Young Families

Contents

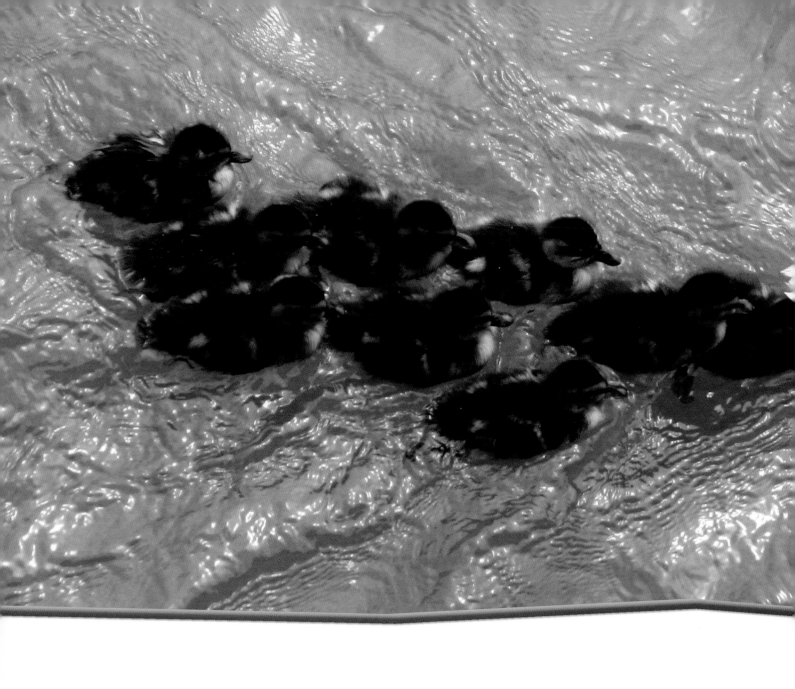

Chapter 1
A Duckling Grows Up

Wild Words

A male duck is called a **drake**. *A female duck is called a* **hen**. *A hen lays a group of eggs called a* **clutch**. *The babies that hatch are called* **ducklings**.

Baby Duck first heard Mama Duck's voice when he was still inside an egg.

The egg was four weeks old. Mama Duck had kept it warm all that time by sitting on it—as well as eight other eggs! Now it was time for the eggs to hatch. Mama Duck could hear her babies peeping inside them.

Baby Duck's egg was the first egg laid by Mama Duck, so it was the first one to hatch. Baby Duck chipped a series of holes around one end of the egg with his bill. Then he pushed with his head, feet, and tiny wings until the shell broke open.

Baby Duck tumbled out. He was sopping wet—and very tired. He sat and dozed as his baby feathers dried. The other eggs began cracking open around him.

The baby ducks were fluffy and dry when they were just half a day old. By the next morning, they could walk and run. They were ready to leave the nest.

Pipsqueak!

A duckling inside an egg has a hard bump on its upper bill called an egg tooth. It uses the egg tooth to peck holes in its shell from the inside. This is called pipping. The duckling loses the egg tooth a few days after it hatches.

Mama Duck gave a quack that meant, "Follow me!" Then she marched out of the nest and through the long grass. The baby ducks followed. The little parade of ducks traveled all the way to the edge of a nearby pond.

Plip! Plop! Splash! One by one, the ducklings hopped into the water. They paddled quickly after Mama Duck. Mama Duck led them around the edge of the pond, where the water was shallow.

Baby Duck spied an insect floating on the water. Quickly, he snapped it up with his bill. Then he snapped up another. Soon all the ducklings were busy picking, pecking, and poking in the water to find food.

Day after day, Mama Duck guarded her babies carefully. She looked up often to watch for hawks and gulls. Near the shore, she watched for raccoons. She herded her babies away from deep water, where snapping turtles and big fish lurked.

If Mama Duck spied danger, she quacked an alarm. She used different calls for different dangers. Some calls sent Baby Duck and his siblings hurrying close to shore, where they sat still as statues. Other calls made them rush to Mama Duck and crowd around her.

One day, a fox came near the ducklings as they napped on shore. Mama Duck flew close to the fox, then flopped to the ground. She acted as if she had a broken wing. The fox followed her as she flapped and fell, flapped and fell. When she had led the fox far from her babies, she quickly flew up into the air and returned to her family.

Beak Deal!

Both male and female mallard ducklings look a lot like their mother when they are about 6 weeks old. But their bills give them away! Males have greenish bills. Females have orange bills.

Baby Duck and his brothers and sisters looked like fluffy yellow-and-brown pom-poms for about two weeks. Then patches of light-gray down appeared. The ducklings also grew bigger. They now weighed four times as much as they did after hatching.

Baby Duck's soft, fluffy down kept him toasty warm. When it rained, Mama Duck spread her broad wings. The ducklings huddled under these feathery umbrellas to stay dry.

When he was four weeks old, stiff feathers sprouted along Baby Duck's back. He also grew feathers on his sides and his tail.

For a few weeks, Baby Duck looked clumsy and ragged. He was an odd-looking bundle of scraggly down mixed with feathers. His feet were huge and his wings were tiny.

But now he could do most of the things Mama Duck could do. He knew how to tip upside down in the water to find plants to eat. He knew how to groom his feathers. Soon, his wing feathers would start to grow. Baby Duck flapped his stubby wings, practicing for the big day when he would learn to fly.

That big day was coming soon. Baby Duck will be nearly full grown when he turns eight weeks old. He will start to fly. Until then, Baby Duck will stay close to his family.

Chapter 2
A Duck's Body

"Greenhead" is a nickname for the mallard and no wonder. It comes from the shimmering green feathers on the male mallard's head.

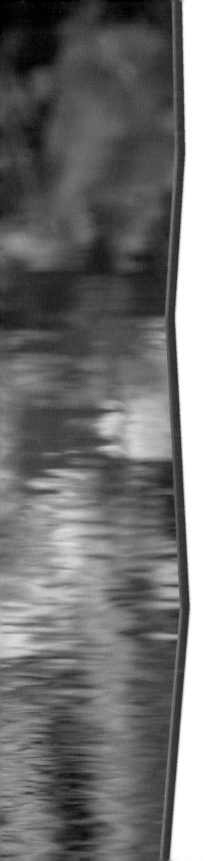

Filling the Bills

A mallard has a flat, broad bill. At the tip of the upper bill is a blunt hook called a nail. The nail helps the duck pick up food or pull up grass that it wants to add to a nest.

Along the edges of the bill are thin ridges called lamellae (pronounced *luh MEH lee*). The lamellae help the duck strain tiny bits of food from the water. The duck moves its tongue to pump water through its bill. The water flows from the bill's tip and out the sides, while the lamellae catch and hold seeds, tiny insects, and other tidbits. A mallard can also strain food from mud with its bill.

Many other kinds of ducks have similar bills. These bills are useful for feeding on the water's surface. Ducks that dive underwater to hunt for fish have longer, thinner bills with jagged edges for gripping slippery prey.

His and Hers

An adult male mallard's bill is yellow or olive green. An adult female's bill is orange splashed with black. She is the one who makes the loud *quack-quack*. The male makes a quieter *rab-rab* sound.

Duck Feet

A mallard, like other ducks, has four toes on each big foot. One toe points backward. The other three toes point forward. These three toes are joined together by flaps of skin called webbing.

Webbed toes help a duck swim when it paddles its feet. As each foot moves back in the water, the toes spread wide. This stretches out the webbing and turns the foot into a wide, strong paddle that pushes against the water. When the foot moves forward, the toes curl and the webbing folds up. This lets the foot move quickly.

On land, a duck's short legs and big feet tend to make it waddle as it walks. A mallard's legs are near the middle of its body, so it does not waddle a lot. Ducks that dive deeply for food have legs set farther back, closer to their tails. These legs help diving ducks swim underwater but make them waddle a lot more than mallards on land.

In a Flap

A mallard's wings measure about three feet from tip to tip when they are spread wide. These broad wings are powered by strong chest muscles. Together, they make the mallard a strong flier. It can leap from the water's surface straight up into the air by flapping fast and hard. Once in flight, it can zip along at speeds up to 40 miles per hour— about as fast as a racehorse can run.

This female mallard is showing off the purple-blue patches on her wings. Male mallards have the same patches. A male duck shows off his patches when he is looking for a mate.

Roll With It!

A duck's waterproof feathers most likely inspired the phrase used to describe people who are not easily upset. They are said to let troubles roll off their backs like water rolls off a duck's back.

A male and female mallard look nothing like each other for most of the year.

A Duck's Feathers

A mallard is covered with about 10,000 feathers. Some of the feathers are strong, stiff, flight feathers. Others are fluffy feathers, called down, that keep the duck warm. Soft feathers cover the duck's head and body. They form a smooth surface that air slips over easily.

Feathers waterproof a duck. Water does not soak into a mallard's feathers. Instead, water forms beads on the feathers and rolls off.

Mr. and Mrs. Mallard

It's usually easy to tell a male and a female mallard apart. A male mallard has a shiny green head. His breast is a rich brown. His sides and belly are pale gray. Four black tail feathers curl up, earning him the nickname "curly-tail."

A female mallard is not brightly colored. Her drab colors make her blend in with the grasses, helping her to fool predators. This blending is called camouflage.

In late summer, male ducks replace their old feathers with new ones. This process is called molting. The new feathers are mostly brown and gray. For a short time, the male looks a lot like the female. By fall, many of these feathers will be replaced by brightly colored ones. Female mallards molt each year, too, but their new feathers always look the same as their old ones.

Chapter 3
Ducks in the Water

Plucky Ducks
Mallards sometimes visit places where people live. They waddle into backyards to eat spilled seed from birdfeeders and swim in wading pools!

A mallard does not need to run across the water when it wants to take off into the air. It can burst into flight from the water in one leap. That's one reason a mallard can live on a small pond in a city park.

Puddle Ducks

An animal's habitat offers food, a home, and a safe place to raise young. Mallards find what they need in habitats with shallow water, such as ponds, lakes, and marshes. They also flock to prairie potholes, which are shallow holes that contain water in grasslands. Some potholes fill up in spring with rain and melting snow, while others are full of water most of the year.

Mallards live in shallow water because they feed at the water's surface and along its edges. They share their habitat with other kinds of ducks that feed in shallow water.

Ducks that dive deeply for food usually live in habitats with deep water and wide-open areas of water to use as runways! They must run across the water's surface while flapping their wings to take off.

Dry Duck

Mallards also need dry land. They usually sleep on land and nest there, too. Female mallards often build nests a short walk away from the water. These places that are near but not on the water are called uplands. In uplands, females look for spots that are thick with grass or other plants in order to hide their nests.

Fowl Food

Mallards eat both plant and animal food. Plant foods include seeds, nuts, wild rice, and grain from farmers' crops. Mallards also eat tiny plants that float in the water. One floating plant is called duckweed because it is such a favorite of ducks! Mallards also dig up and eat short, thick plant stems called tubers.

Mallards eat lots of animal food in spring. They gobble up snails, shrimp, worms, tadpoles, and insects. They also eat fish eggs—and fish, too, if they are able to catch them. Ducklings eat large amounts of animal food during their first month of life. They need the protein to grow.

Ducks in Muck

If you watch mallards, chances are you will see one dunk its head underwater, leaving just its back end sticking out. This is one of the mallard's feeding positions. It is called tipping-up. A mallard tips up when it wants to reach food underwater.

Sometimes, mallards look as if they are nibbling the water's surface. What they are really doing is straining water through their bills to filter out (separate) tiny bits of food. Ducks that feed in this way are called dabbling ducks.

Mallards also feed on land. In winter, they often flock to farmlands to eat spilled grain and other bits left behind after the crops have been collected.

What is this upside-down mallard doing underwater? A tipped-up mallard may be straining mud on the bottom through its bill. It may be yanking up plants. A mallard may even push its whole head into the muck to pull up a tuber.

The mallard's neck is so long that the duck can reach almost every part of its body with its bill to clean its feathers. The mallard uses its feet to scratch the base of its neck and its head.

Cleaning and Preening

A mallard spends about two hours a day taking care of its feathers.

Feather care starts with a bath. Although a duck spends much time in the water, it does not get wet! This is because its feathers shed water. The duck must make an effort to get wet! A bathing duck quickly dips its head in the water and flaps its wings, splashing water into the air. It ruffles its feathers to let water trickle through them.

After a few dunks, the duck moves to a dry spot. It beats its wings and shakes its body, spraying water from itself like a wet dog. Then it begins to groom its feathers. This grooming is called preening.

A duck preens by running its feathers through its bill. First, it clamps its bill on the bottom of a feather (the part nearest the skin). Then it runs the feather through its bill until it reaches the tip. This action removes dirt. It also tidies up the thin fibers of each feather. The fibers, called barbs, zip together and form a smooth surface that keeps water out when a duck swims.

Preening may also include oiling the feathers with a thick liquid made by the duck's oil gland. The oil gland is a little knob just above its tail. The duck uses its bill to take oil from the gland and then spread it over its feathers. The oil helps keep the feathers soft and flexible. Scientists think the oil may also kill harmful kinds of fungus that can infect a duck's skin and feathers.

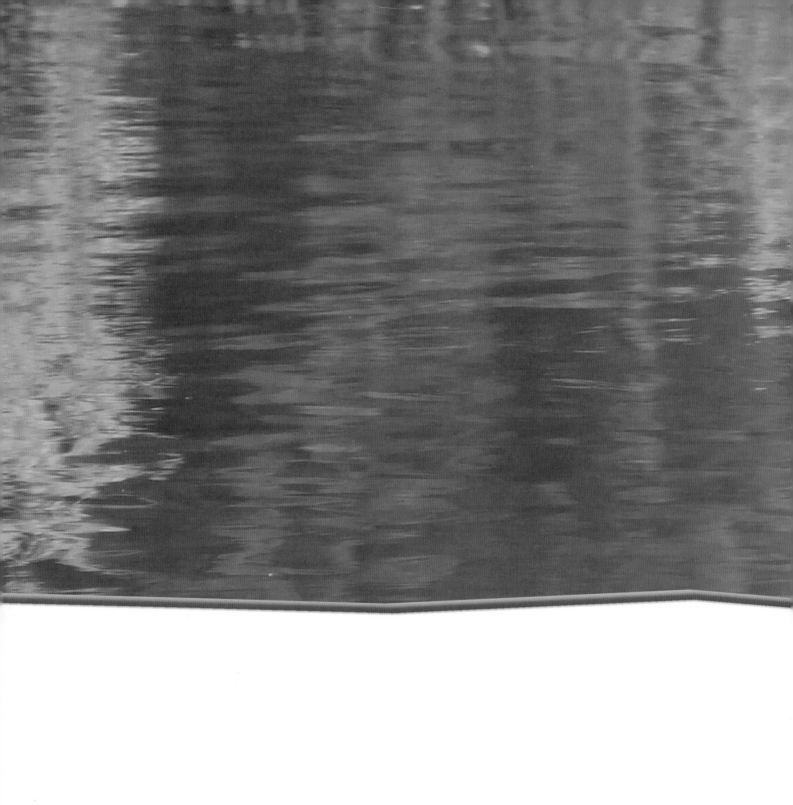

Chapter 4
A Duck's Year

When a female has chosen a mate, she lets him know it by tossing her head and calling.

Cuddle Ducks!

Male and female mallards form pairs during fall and winter. They move and call in special ways to attract a mate. These are called courtship displays. Small groups of males surround a female to court her with signals that mean "Pick me!"

A mallard male uses different displays when courting. He grunts, whistles, shakes his head, and lift his wings and tail to show off his fine feathers. The female swims and nods her head to encourage the drakes to display.

Finding a Home

When the ice melts on ponds and lakes in late winter, mallards return from warmer places. The first flocks to arrive are made up of many pairs of ducks. Soon the flocks break up as each pair gets busy finding a place to live.

The female mallard chooses the nest site. She and her mate land when she spies a likely spot. Then she waddles through the grass, quacking as she goes. Her quacks may help her find out where predators are in the area. Quacking also warns other females not to pick nest sites too close to hers.

All the while, the female's mate waits for her. His job is to guard her—not just from predators but also from drakes without mates that may try to court her.

The Best Nest

The female finally settles on a place for her nest. It is usually a spot just a short waddle from the water, hidden in the grass.

She begins building her nest by scraping the ground with her feet. As she scrapes, she turns slowly while pressing her belly against the ground. A shallow bowl forms in the soil and grass.

The first egg is laid inside this bowl. Each morning, the female adds another egg. As she sits on the nest, she reaches out and pulls up blades of grass around her to help hide the nest. She plucks soft down feathers from her breast and tucks them into the nest, too.

Egged On

The female does not sit on her eggs all day long until she has laid the last one. Now she is ready to stay on the nest and keep the eggs warm with the heat from her body. Sitting on eggs in this way is called incubating.

As the female incubates, she turns the eggs over now and then. She leaves the nest for just an hour or two each day to feed and preen.

Incubation lasts about 28 days. The ducklings are able to walk soon after hatching. Their mother leads them to water to feed and swim. The family no longer needs the nest.

What a Site!
Not all mallards nest in grassy places. If a female is in a wooded area instead of grassland, she may nest under a fallen log or even in a tree. Some females nest right on the shore among tall water plants.

Wherever a female chooses to nest, a body of water is never very far away.

Last-Minute Mallards!

In many places mallards wait until the last minute to migrate! Even ducks living in the farthest north may hang around until late November, or even until ice actually forms on lakes and ponds. Many mallards that live in places where winter is not freezing cold do not migrate at all, while some mallards fly as far south as Mexico.

Time to Leave

Once the female starts sitting on her eggs, the male's job is done. His bright colors could attract predators, so he can't stay near. The female doesn't need his help raising the ducklings, either. The pair splits up and the male takes off.

No-Fly Zone

In early summer, the male mallard molts. He grows a set of brown feathers as his brightly colored feathers fall out. He also molts his wing feathers. For almost a month, he cannot fly. A female molts her wing feathers later, after her ducklings have grown up.

Time to Fly South

By autumn, mallards are ready to fly again. Moving from a breeding place to a place to spend the winter is called migration.

Mallards can survive in cold weather, but they can't stay in a place where the water freezes or snow covers their food. They must migrate to places where they can find food and open water.

Chapter 5
Ducks in the World

White ducks and yellow ducklings that are often seen on farms are descendents of wild mallards.

Mallards Everywhere

Of all the different kinds of ducks in the world, mallards are the most common. They live in more parts of the world than any other kind of dabbling duck. They breed in North America, Europe, and Asia. Some mallards migrate to parts of Africa and Southeast Asia for the winter.

Mallards are able to live in so many different places because they are very adaptable—they find food and shelter in a variety of habitats. This is partly because they eat a wide variety of foods. Mallards also adapt to being near people. They are able to live and raise their young even with humans using their habitat, too.

Farm Ducks

The mallard is the ancestor of most tame ducks raised on farms. Over time, farm-raised ducks began to look different from their wild ancestors because people picked which ducks to breed. Scientists call this process domestication.

Today, domestic ducks come in an amazing variety of sizes and shapes—from tiny, chubby ones to tall "runner ducks" that are sometimes referred to as bowling pins with legs!

The Future of Mallards

The biggest threat to mallards is the same one faced by other water birds: loss of habitat. In the past 100 years, many grasslands and wetlands have been turned into land for farms and buildings. As a result, mallards and other birds have fewer places to feed and nest.

In 1986, the United States and Canada set up the North American Waterfowl Management Plan. Part of the plan called for repairing habitats that had been harmed. New areas were also set aside for water birds. Other programs help keep prairie potholes available for ducks. Still others urge farmers to turn average farmland into excellent duck habitat. Many people are working hard to preserve habitats for mallards and other ducks.

Fast Facts About Mallards

Scientific name	*Anas platyrhynchos*
Class	Aves
Order	Anseriformes
Size	Males to 25 inches long Females to 23 inches long
Weight	Males to 2.75 pounds Females to 2.5 pounds
Life span	7-15 years in the wild (record is 29 years)
Habitat	Wetlands, lakes, ponds
Speed	About 40 miles per hour

Between 9 and 10 million mallards live in North America during the breeding season.

Glossary of Wild Words

camouflage colors and patterns on an animal that help it blend in with its surroundings

clutch a nest of eggs

dabbling feeding by straining water and mud through the bill

down soft, fluffy feathers that keep a bird warm

duckling a baby duck

drake a male duck

habitat the natural environment where an animal or plant lives

hatch to be born by breaking out of an egg

hen a female duck

incubation the time spent keeping eggs warm until they are ready to hatch

lamellae grooves and ridges along the edges of a duck's bill that filter food from water and mud

migration	going from one place to another at certain times of the year to find food or to mate and give birth	**range**	all the places where a species lives
molting	shedding old feathers and having new ones grow in	**species**	a group of living things that are the same in many ways
predator	an animal that hunts and eats other animals to survive	**tipping-up**	feeding by turning upside down in the water to reach the bottom
preening	cleaning and grooming feathers with the bill	**tuber**	a short, thick plant stem that grows underground
prey	animals that are hunted by other animals for food	**wetlands**	areas with much water in the soil, such as swamps, marshes, and bogs

Index